CW00970289

~

CLIMBING STILES

A Wander Through the
Countryside & Beyond

~

CHARLIE BENNETT

~

Also by the author:

Down The Rabbit Hole:
The Misadventures of an Unlikely Naturalist

Charlie Bennett
www.charliebennettauthor.co.uk

~

~

Charlie Bennett is a farmer, writer,
and passionate advocate for the countryside.
He is joint owner of Middleton North, a
farm near Morpeth in Northumberland,
North East England. Here, he works to
support existing wildlife and attract new
species alongside sustainable stock farming
designed to add to the diversity of flora and
fauna in the area. Charlie and his family live
on the farm with their two labradors, Ella and
Frog, and their polymath terrier Dotty,
who Charlie maintains is the brains behind
the whole operation.

~

Text © Charlie Bennett, 2024

Illustrations © Charlie Bennett, 2024

Edited, designed and typeset by Jane Pikett

All rights reserved. Without limiting the rights under copyright reserved above, no part of this publication may be reproduced, stored in a retrieval system, or transmitted in any form or by any means, electronic, mechanical, photocopying, recording or otherwise, without the prior written permission of the copyright owner and the publisher of this book.

Published by Curlicue

Curlicue Publishing is an imprint of The Editor, a division of Creation id Ltd, registered in England.

A CIP record for this book is available from the British Library.

This book is set in:

Minion Pro Regular 11.5pt/18pt/25pt

Apple Chancery Regular 20pt

ISBN: 978-1-0685414-1-4

Printed and bound by Imprint Digital, Exeter, UK

Curlicue
ENGLAND

CLIMBING STILES

A Wander Through the
Countryside & Beyond

~

CHARLIE BENNETT

~

Charlie Bennett's stories about his farm, wildlife and the wider world are whimsical, vivid and at times exquisitely reflective. This collection is the second book of tales which began as Charlie's popular columns published in *The Northumbrian*, a countryside magazine which focuses on the people and places of Northumberland, in North East England. In each edition of the magazine, Charlie relates stories of life on his farm and beyond. On his land, he aims to bring together sustainable farming and wildlife in a model he calls common-sense farming. His wanderings through the countryside also have him musing on the people in his life and the world in which we live, his stories combining gentle humour, reflection, and insight into the struggles facing humankind and nature in existing side by side and in harmony today.

~

For Charlotte, Edward and Milo

Contents

~

~

It's a Magical Life

You may or may not know that this is my second book. The first one, *Down The Rabbit Hole*, came from a fissure that opened in my mind when I became an early adopter of Covid.

You'll be either delighted or horrified to hear that the creative tap hasn't turned off in the years since the pandemic. In fact, my imagination seems to have expanded during this time, and it continues to be forever casting new stories for my fingers to craft on the keyboard.

Inspiration is a funny thing. It comes in the dead of night, when I'm out on a walk, leafing through a magazine, or chatting to people on the train. All these experiences go into the mixer that is my mind and a day or two, even months later, a story starts telling me to stop everything and let it go free.

This book is different from the last one in that as well as my beloved wildlife, my relationships with you, my fellow inhabitants of this green and pleasant land, play a larger role than they have previously. Be it dealing with daemons, pondering on retirement, or just looking back on my childhood and the people who have influenced me from there on in.

It is a crazy world we live in, but I honestly believe it remains a magical one. I hope these stories will help you to realise that, too.

Charlie Bennett
October 2024

ONE

Climbing Stiles

Climbing a stile has been the beginning of many of my adventures. In Kirkby Overblow, the village in Yorkshire where I grew up, there are two rather nice stiles built of dressed stone which sit snuggly between beautiful dry stone walls.

Stone steps on either side lead to two parallel iron bars which stop sheep or cattle escaping from the fields. Over many years, these bars have become worn as people's wellies have caught on them as they have climbed over, usually led by dogs whose tummies have rubbed on the bars as they have clambered or jumped to the other side. Thus they have acquired a burnished bronze finish which is pleasing to the touch.

I learnt a rhyme you may know beside one of these stiles. It goes: *"Run a mile jump a stile, or eat a country pancake."* The rhyme was used to pick people for various games we played as children, and for some reason, us village kids used to hang around one of the stiles when we were planning our escapades.

At one time, we got into a craze of collecting old keys, eventually all of us clanking around the village like miniature jailers. One day, Guy Barrett found a big key. Musing over this at the stile, somebody wondered if it would fit the lock for the village shop's store shed. In our world, this rickety old wooden building was akin to Fort Knox, and within it Mr Parkin, the whistling shopkeeper, kept boxes and boxes of sweets.

With lookouts placed, we sneaked SAS-style down the side of the shop. The key was placed in the lock and with a satisfying clunk it opened. We stood on the threshold surveying mountains of Mars bars, Sherbet Dips, Penny Arrows, Marathons and – well, you name it, it was there. Then, as one, we concluded this heist had proved too easy, so we re-locked the door and snuck off. I have played that moment over in my mind many times over the years and am always delighted to think that the kids of Kirkby Overblow shared a strong and unquestionable moral compass. Alternatively, we might have been full of scrumped apples.

Back at the stiles, we had options. The bottom stile led down a field at one side of which an ancient wood stands to this day. Within the wood were dilapidated old buildings and exciting dells to explore. The problem for us, however, was that this was the domain of Ferret, the Game Keeper – the sort of man whose bottom buttons on his waistcoat had never met their eyes on the farther side of several acres of tattersall check shirt.

If Ferret spotted you, his face would turn a satisfyingly vivid purple and he'd come after you like an angry gorilla (I don't blame him – we were messing about in his best pheasant drive). Bellowing with rage, he would thunder: "Booger off ye leetle baastads . . . I'll tell yer dads . . ." We loved this, as the reaction was guaranteed every time and thankfully he never caught us, though we did fear the rumours of man-traps. However, we did get BIKs (Bollockings in the Kitchen) on our return home, as Ferret was as good as his word.

The top stile had its treats, too. This one led – still leads – from a thin, wiggly road called Dawson Lane. Once over the stile you follow a path on the edge of a field where in my day very smart, expensive horses eyed you haughtily, doubtless thinking, "what are those little ragamuffins up to now?" Well, I can tell you – we were heading for the graveyard.

Once through a garden, the path leads to another stile, this one possibly even older than the other two. It has big stone steps and rather than bars a sweet little lychgate on the top. We loved the graveyard. Around the church is a concrete trench that prevents the higher-level ground at the back of the building resting on the walls. This was perfect for enacting D-Day or World War One battles. We were obsessed with playing armies; unsurprisingly so, as many of our parents had been kids in the Second World War and our grandparents had either fought in it or endured it.

For small boys, this connection to the war was well-catered for. Trash mags like *Commando* taught you elementary German like "hande hoch!" (hands up) and "donner und blitzen" (thunder and lightning), which were stock phrases of our daily lives. They also instructed us in how to behave in difficult situations without swearing, as in: "Dang, Sarge – it looks like I've copped one in the leg . . ."

Our military operations were carried out with respect for the church and its graveyard. Most of us had been christened there and we'd seen the usual hatches, matches, and dispatches of our respective families take place within its walls. That said, we were fascinated by some of the graves, including those marked not by a simple stone, but by neat stone boxes with the name of the deceased lovingly carved into a slab on top.

One of them had a gap just under the lid, presumably caused by erosion. One day Ian Richardson and I plucked up the courage to shine a torch through the gap. We were expecting to see a skeleton, as we thought that's how these stone boxes worked. However, what we thought we saw was equally disturbing. Through the dry, greyish soil inside poked a withered, scaly hand with what looked like talons for fingernails. I have never run so fast in my life.

I remember nervously chewing over this find with Ian later. However, what I don't know is if this story has grown arms and legs in the 50 years since it happened. I suspect it has, but I still wouldn't look back in that hole today for all the tea in China.

While thinking about this story I made a list
of other stiles I have crossed, including one in
the dark in Somerset, where I spent most of a
night crossing and re-crossing the same stile.
I'd been to the pub. What could that have to do
with it?

More recently, I have delighted in the huge
ladder-like stiles in Northumberland which
cross 6ft stone walls, and the neat little ones you
sometimes find along Hadrian's Wall. Perhaps
you will have your own favourites. In my mind,
they act as portals to revisit old adventures and
memories, or help to create new ones. So if you
see a stile on your travels, either climb over it
or shore it up in your memory – I guarantee
wonders await you on the other side.

~

TWO

Getting to know Your Daemons

I often wonder why certain animals have such a profound effect on me. The closest I've come to explain it lies in Philip Pullman's *Dark Materials* trilogy. In this series of books, every character has an animal alter-ego known as their daemon. These animals are of the opposite sex to their character and often act as their human's moral compass and voice of reason. Plus, if the character is separated from their daemon, they die.

A visceral connection to a wild creature – is such a thing possible? I think it is. But before we dive into my personal daemons, some advice on finding your own. We are encouraged these days to get out into nature. This is excellent advice, but I fear this sometimes takes the form of an 'experience', or a day out. That is, something you can ring-fence in your diary. But to get really close to nature, you need to go deeper. This requires time and the ability to switch off from the everyday.

An example – in mid-summer I like to get up early to go and sit by one of the ponds on our farm. It's important to be comfortable, so I take an old coat to sit on and a flask of coffee. Often, the morning starts misty, the sun that has never really gone to bed lighting the sky a burnt orange. A few birds will start up – sedge warblers whistling and popping, skylarks calling to mates from on high, the distinctive "*it's awful, it's awful . . .*" of a wood pigeon parading on the branch of an old oak.

the more it becomes muscle memory, so does reading water. Fellow fishermen will describe a river as 'fishy' in spring. Press them and they may initially struggle to explain themselves, but push a little and they will dig into their subconscious to explain that riverside plants are developing, the colour of the water is changing and becoming (this might just be in my mind) more 'sparkly', and early insects are beginning to emerge on warmer days.

Another power – our innate hunter-gatherer – is also at work here. Generations going back as far as we have eaten fish and game have known when it is time to hunt a chosen prey, which is why the 17,000-year-old cave paintings in Lascaux, France, represent a calendar of which animals are ready to hunt at which times of the year.

So, I am wired to the ways of the river, and this brings a stillness, an ability to move quietly, a sixth sense of what might be ahead. Last year, I was trout fishing on the River Lyd in Devon. This is a beautiful river in a deep valley surrounded by ancient cow pastures with gnarled old trees dotted along its banks. This makes for tricky casting, but if you get into the water quietly, a short cast is often possible. The trout are wild, coiled on hair triggers, which means that the slightest suspicion of danger and they're gone.

On this occasion, as I approached a pool on a bend, my senses told me something was up. Electricity sharpening my mind, I crept around some rushes, my senses telling me, 'go slow, something's there, you just haven't seen it yet'. Then there she was – a sow otter. (This is the most un-pig like creature on earth, but the female is a sow and the male is a boar, which are lazy nomenclatures in my book. More of an elegant hen or a beautiful mare, perhaps?)

My otter was busy catching crayfish, diving down and no doubt turning stones over with her dexterous fingers to grasp her prey, which is no mean feat, as crayfish have vicious pincers. She then brought her prize to an island of driftwood to gobble it up. I watched, transfixed, for I don't how long. That's the joy of daemon watching – time is a human-made construct and evaporates when you're immersed in nature. Eventually, I withdrew quietly, the otter's feeding more important than my fishing, and sat down in a sunny spot to commit the experience to memory.

This is one of many otter encounters. Like the swallow and the roe deer, the otter has a physical pull on my heart. Why? Well, its physicality is amazing – sinuous, fast, and tenacious. And it has a friendly face – curious and canny. It is also accomplished at fishing. Fly-fishing is a difficult occupation, done above the surface, trying, as described above, to read the runes of what lies beneath, and it takes great practice to decipher the messages and hopefully catch a fish. The otter probably does all that too, but it can also enter the fishy realm underwater, where it is in its element. Yes, it's good being human, but I'd give a lot to be an otter for a day.

Where does this leave us? Well, it reminds me how much I crave these experiences with my daemons, and the sense of wellbeing which follows. So if you get the chance, find yourself a quiet spot and switch off. This can take time and practice, but I promise that amazing things will happen, and in time you will have your own daemons to cherish.

~

THREE

Nutty as a Fruitcake

It has been suggested that I am as mad as a box of frogs or as barmy as a badger. These comments have probably been accurately aimed, as my behaviour is not always conventional. I have a passion for chocolate peanuts that I can eat faster than Usain Bolt on the 100m; I often wear a hat in bed; and I have a 51-year old Land Rover that I have asked to be buried in when I die (either that, or for my ashes to be fired out of a friend's cannon).

Sadly, beneath these eccentricities, I have also had (as Winston Churchill described) a number of visits from the black dogs. In modern parlance, that is depression and anxiety. Luckily, because it is the 21st century and I am a modern man (the current Mrs Bennett has just sprayed her coffee across the kitchen table), I have been able to find help with this.

You might know that in farming my mantra is common sense, which is a great commodity, if often hard to find. Any road, on one occasion when I got the blues (again), both common sense and some good friends said to me: "Get some help," and this I did, because it was common sense. If my Land Rover breaks down, I do sometimes fix it, but this often makes it worse. Better that my trusty garageist waves the spanners and twiddles the thingummybobs so that Lawrence (that is the vehicle's name) is ready to ride again.

So, when my noggin went on the blink I went to a therapist. She was amazing. We got to the root of my anxiety, worked through some therapy that was both verbal and physical, and in not too many weeks I was just about back to normal. The thing is, I'll never be perfect, just like Lawrence, but now at least I know the symptoms when the bats are coming home to roost and I can put things in place to weather the storm.

One of the best physical things to do when you have had a bad turn, or are indeed having one, is go for a walk. I find the countryside best, but I also love a wander round the streets of London, Newcastle, Haltwhistle or wherever, as walking and people-watching is a great tonic. However, for this journey we are going to focus on the countryside.

It has been proven by the boffinery that walking in fresh air is therapeutic, and this works even better if you can also be among nature and plants. Furthermore, sleep specialists have found that green light from trees and plants helps us get to sleep at night. So, I was out one day, getting my fill of all these goodies, when I spotted three roe deer bouncing into the undergrowth. (As an aside, why do they have white bottoms? It's a bit like that Gary Larson cartoon of a deer with a target on his chest and his friend saying to him, "Bummer of a birth mark, Hal . . ." Wouldn't they be better being brown all over? Though I guess it does tell other deer in the herd, "we're off sharpish and you should come too . . .").

These animals were reacting to stress. Seeing a man with dogs is often not a good thing for deer; though my dogs now know they will generally not get anywhere near, so just give them a glance as if to say: "I could catch you, but I can't be chewed."

The deer also know this and run just far enough away to know they are out of harm's way. This short trot, however, is often more complex than it looks. Roe deer are territorial and spend time working out escape routes. You know that thing when you do something 10,000 times and you develop muscle memory, so your body can do it automatically? Concert pianists, for example. Or finding the loo in the middle of the night in the dark. Except when you're staying with someone else, forget where you are, enter your host's bedroom and turn the light on . . .

Well, our deer are well-versed in not getting the wrong room. In fact, precisely the opposite: they are wired to get away safely automatically, so when they sense danger, their stress does exactly what it does to us; it puts them into flight and fight mode. But their advantage is that they are going down an escape route without having to think about it.

I'm pretty sure lots of creatures do this. Hares will almost mirror the roe deer's behaviour, and have another trick up their sleeve that they share with the mighty vole – they can sit stock still. Movement-spotting predators are often bewildered, as their prey has for all intents and purposes disappeared. Birds like pheasants will also do this or scarper as fast as their wings will carry them, squawking like a banshee to tell everyone else that Fred Fox is on the prowl.

But what of the predators? Life at the top of the evolutionary tree is not always a bed of roses, as other critters often share the perch with you or might even occupy a branch above. I have noticed this with the aforementioned fox. At the sight of danger, as often as not they go into slink mode. Lowering their profile, and quiet as a barn owl, they will slink into the undergrowth where they may find a hole to have a snooze in until the trouble has passed and their anxiety has had a chance to melt away.

Other creatures use teamwork to deal with stress. Murmurations of birds or shoals of fish are bundles of the same species, often in huge numbers. When trouble appears in the form of a peregrine falcon or a dolphin, they start moving as one to try to dazzle the hunter out of taking any of their throng.

It is cleverly done. For example, I have explained before that starlings copy the behaviour of the birds immediately around them. In doing so, smoke-like patterns evolve and predators are often left flummoxed.

That is instinct, but I would argue that we have the same skills. They may lie hidden, as today you are unlikely to be eaten by a sabre-toothed tiger or chased by an angry mammoth (it does happen, but not often in Hartburn). But the modern stresses of life, if not addressed, can cause anxiety and depression, and these are not nice places to go.

Funnily enough, like the animals I have discussed, help is at hand from our fellow humans. The time, particularly for men of my age (57, if you wondered), to "man-up" and get a stiff upper lip are over. That behaviour can lead to a dark place where the monsters you thought as a child lived under your bed really hang out. So my advice is that if you are in the dumps or have the blues, or are wracked by the vice-like grip of anxiety, then for goodness sake get some help.

Where, might you ask? If you are local to me, try Idos in Newcastle-upon-Tyne. They will give you traditional medical help but also some have alternatives like the therapy I received –

sleep advice, yoga, or you might even be sent on
a walk with me, in which case, bring stout boots
and plenty of chocolate peanuts.

~

FOUR

Why Aye, Pet

My first pet was called Mickey. He was a rather handsome russet guinea pig. I think I'd wanted a mouse, but as the youngest of four, any present (especially a furry one) was very welcome. Anyway, Mickey made extremely pleasing noises and was fun to have around.

Not long after he arrived, it was time for the Weeton Show. Held in early summer, it was like events of its type throughout the country – tents smelling of dead grass full of jam and stick dressers; joyful children towed around on a tarpaulin behind a tractor; and various animal judging competitions. These ranged from ruddy-faced farmers in their best tweed parading prize sheep and cattle, to the other end of the spectrum, the pet competition, into which it was decided that I should enter Mickey.

The great day arrived and I spent considerable time combing my pet, making sure he looked his best. He seemed to take all this in good heart and let out a few satisfied whistles as the Action Man comb brought his fur to a conker-like glossiness.

I didn't expect him to win, but I thoroughly enjoyed taking part and spent at least five minutes answering searching questions from the judge, Colonel Strangely-Brown, who had nearly as many whiskers as Mickey. He moved on to inspect dogs, cats, tortoises and budgies and Mickey and I wandered off. Later, my red-faced sister found us loitering around the sweet stall. "Quick, Charlie, come back to the judging tent!" she cried, where to my surprise Mickey had won first prize. We were paraded in front of the local press, Mickey sitting on a huge silver salver with me grinning toothlessly behind him.

I next saw this trophy at school the following Monday morning. The headmaster was clutching it at the front of our classroom and my stomach balled up at the thought of being called up to have Mickey's achievement celebrated. But then the headmaster's face clouded and his eyebrows (which at the best of times resembled a pair of huge hairy caterpillars) collided at the sight of the citation. The winner of the 1972 Weeton Show pet prize was engraved for all eternity as Mrs BE Bennett, and she wasn't a pupil in Class 1A.

I guess the engraver simply put the name of the person paying for the class entry on the salver, and that was my mum. Years later, my niece won the same trophy, and I laughed it off stoically when she spotted granny's name for 1972. But after 51 years ruminating on this injustice, I am of the firm opinion that it should be the name Mickey, the squeaky russet guinea pig, that was engraved on that plate.

After my prize-winning guinea pig, I progressed to larger pets. My first dog was called Ginger (you can guess why). His mother Dinah, our dog, had a litter of nine puppies and my mother was rightly keen to get them sold. However, I was not letting Ginger go, so I scooped him up and locked myself in the loo with him. My mother kindly relented and I was allowed to keep him. He was a great dog, full of life, excellent company for a young boy, and particularly good at smiling when he was happy, which he did by tucking his top lips under his canines.

Probably his greatest skill was fishing. Once, sitting on the beach in Norfolk scoffing Cheddars washed down with orange squash, he appeared out of the waves holding in his mouth a huge fish that was still flapping. I can't remember if we ate it, but I wouldn't be surprised if we did.

WHY AYE, PET

Since Ginger, we have had numerous dogs and our current three are building up their own wealth of stories. But I'd like to focus on probably our most famous dog, a border terrier called Reg. My mother-in-law's family have been breeding borders since God was a boy. Indeed, one grandfather had 30 (we have a photo of him sitting in a chair wearing half of them), and Reg was one of the descendants of this family.

Sadly, his first owner hadn't been able to keep him, so my wife and I took him on. It didn't take him long to start building his reputation. On his first night with us I took him for a walk on Clapham Common. Unbeknown to me, his previous owner had given him little or no training, and in a two-year-old terrier with a will of his own, this was bad news.

As soon as I let him off the lead, he was off, making straight for an area where, well – what can I say? A place where people like to get to know each other better. I ran in shouting, "Reg, Reg you little [expletive] come here . . ." and suddenly heads started popping up. It appeared that the name Reg might be known to this little community. Red-faced, I turned tail only to find my Reg had moved out of the woods to the pond where he was eyeing up a Canada goose.

This was the start of a long and eventful life into which he jumped with the carefree abandon of a marauding Viking. He was at heart a good egg, so I'm guessing that when he finally shuffled off this mortal coil at the amazing age of 16, he made it to the pearly gates. There, however, Saint Peter doubtless had quite a charge sheet to run through, including chasing squirrels to their demise in Green Park in front of horrified tourists, eating my aunt's favourite hen, and getting stuck down a badger hole, causing my wife to dislocate her shoulder trying to extract him.

There was also chasing all the pheasants from our best drive before it started, me in pursuit employing similar expletives to the aforementioned (my guests said it was the best moment of the day). Reg also once latched onto a boxer dog in Hyde Park, and while he caused no damage, the owner still insisted on a silent taxi journey to a wallet-cooling emergency appointment with her vet.

When Reg went for his meeting with Saint Peter, I buried him in his favourite wood; a place where he had regularly dug up baby rabbits for fun. But rabbits have long memories, and it wasn't long before they in turn dug him up. He is now buried with a large stone on his grave and I smile every time I pass it, often placing a wildflower next to the rabbit droppings.

To round this story off, I'm going to tell you about my latest pet. I'm not sure if the descriptor 'pet' is entirely accurate, as he is a pigeon, thus I don't own him and he doesn't own me. However, I do feed and water him and he seems to listen when I go to talk to him by the bird table.

I have named him Walter. He is huge and waddles more than he walks. He also looks vacant, but he is far from stupid and has worked out that if he leaves the sparrows to mine into the fat balls, he can muscle them out of the way and fill his crop.

I have named him Walter because he looks like a neighbour of ours when I was a kid. He was called Walter Pickard and was a pigeon-shaped man, with a smallish head and round glasses on a round body and shortish legs. He and his wife lived in the cottage next to us. They were kindness personified and when my brother fell ill (I think with the mumps) they looked after him.

During this time, the human Walter passed his extensive knowledge of the sport of kings to my brother and every morning they would religiously study the *Racing Post*, deciding who was going to win the 3.30 at Haydock Park and the like. It soon became clear that my brother Jim, at the tender age of seven, had an eye for a winner, so Walter placed his bets on his new protégé's recommendations and soon they were both in the money. It didn't take my dad long to spot an opportunity, so he started funding the operation, and all was well until my mother got wind of the cartel next door when my brother's new petrol go-kart was delivered.

Actually, I'm not sure how she found out, but she makes Miss Marple look amateurish in the sleuthing stakes. This, and the boy who broke the bank at Monte Carlo recovered from his mumps and returned to school, probably with more valuable life experience than formal education would ever give him.

Walter the pigeon doesn't impart racing tips, but in time he too will have his place on the wall of pet fame, because I know the pets of my life have enriched it to such an extent that I couldn't think of it without them.

~

FIVE

An Abbey Safari

It came to my attention in the writing of this book that in 2024 Hexham Abbey was marking 1,350 years since the first place of worship was founded on its site by Saint Wilfrid.

It is hard today to imagine this busy, living church being that old. 674 was a time of flux – the Romans had left Britain, Christianity was finding its feet, and the country was rife with

AN ABBEY SAFARI

feuding kingdoms – and the Abbey's history since has been at times turbulent. There always seems to have been someone with the intention of dismantling this beautiful building, not least the Vikings and the Scottish raiders, while Henry VIII managed to dissolve it (at least as a monastery). Luckily, some wise soul made the point that the town could use the Abbey as a parish church, so it was left alone. Since then, threats to this place have been more from the weather and the increasing cost of keeping the building standing.

Deciding it was time to pay a proper visit, I arrived on a cold, blustery April morning. It had been a year of endless rain and cold snaps, but the Abbey gardens were alive with birdsong, so I reached for my trusty Merlin. No, this is not a 27-litre Spitfire engine, but an app that identifies the birds singing around you. I recorded chiff chaffs, blackbirds, goldfinches, and a cawing rook, which got me thinking – there's lots of life outside the Abbey, but what could be living within?

CLIMBING STILES

Now, you will have to allow me some licence here. On speaking with the custodians of the Abbey it is clear that very few non-human creatures inhabit the place. If they do, they are small – spiders and their lunch (flies); bats in the belfry; and possibly, when they get the chance, pigeons. But if you include inanimate animals, then a cast of characters as long as your arm appears. There are flocks of lambs, convocations of eagles, herds of deer, troops of monkeys, and a horror of mythical beasts.

Wondering how I might bring this cornucopia of creatures to life for this chapter, David Attenborough, as is often the case, was an inspiration. When he's educating us about the world's jungles, he will often start in the canopy and work his way down to the forest floor, so we're going to board a mini 'copter and make for the Abbey ceiling. This is a long way above when you're standing on the Abbey floor – more than 60ft above, in fact. Our safari starts here among the roof bosses. These are ornamental discs attached where roof trusses join, and they've been elaborately carved since the 1390s. Many of the designs are floral or feature various representations of Christ, saints, and angels. But among them are the creatures we seek, including a lion, a dove, and three fish representing the Holy Trinity.

These are laden with religious symbolism of course, but the pagan also makes an entrance in the shape of a particularly fine Green Man, and this is where we get lost down a new rabbit hole. The question is, why does this pagan symbol appear time and time again in Christian churches? I've found many answers in numerous texts that connect the Green Man to rebirth, the story being that he went to sleep in winter and came back to life in spring. I also think it might have been hard for new Christians to discard their pagan heritage, especially when parallel messages were so obvious.

To descend from the roof a little, the light in Hexham Abbey is magical thanks to its superb stained-glass windows. The glass itself covers a huge time span, ranging from three fragments of Roman glass which originated in Corbridge to the magnificent 21st century triptych Tyrrell window. The stained glass here tells numerous biblical stories and depicts important figures including Saint Andrew, to whom the Abbey is dedicated. The northern saints obviously feature, including Bede, King Oswald, Wilfrid, Queen Etheldreda (who gifted Wilfrid the money and the land to build his church here), and of course Cuthbert.

As you might imagine, the windows also feature quite a collection of characters from the animal kingdom. There are lambs, if not of the gambolling variety because, as you may be aware, in the Bible they seldom make it to sheephood and are usually depicted awaiting departure from this world. Eagles and lions fare better as images of strength, and doves feature as agents of peace.

Many humans like having animals around them. In a church context, they may have symbolic meanings, but often they are represented because we need, and like, their company. A stained-glass depiction of Saint Cuthbert in the Abbey is a fine example, featuring the otters which were famously said to have dried his feet as he emerged from the sea; one of the seals that proliferate around Lindisfarne; and my favourite, the cuddy, or eider duck – the nickname 'cuddy' derived from Cuthbert. Only this weekend, I was watching them dibbling about at Boulmer Bay and noted what fabulous creatures they are.

As we descend feather-like towards the Abbey floor, let's have a look at some of the stone carvings depicting animals. My guide and I spent some time at the tomb of Sir Gilbert de Umfraville, in which the figure of the deceased is surrounded by small creatures. Thousands of hands have worn them down over the years, but there are what may be toads, and possibly a mouse. Sir Gilbert's neighbour, Thomas Tyndale, has a reassuring lion to rest his feet on (I'm definitely ordering one of those for the Bennett tomb). But these animals are just youngsters. At the base of the medieval night stair in the Abbey, you will find the tombstone of a Roman cavalryman named Flavinus.

Its dedication declares: *To the Venerated Departed: Here Lies Flavinus, a Horse Rider of the Cavalry Regiment of Petriana, Standard Bearer of the Troop of Candidus, Aged 25, of 7 Years' Service.* The stone shows Flavinus aboard a magnificent rearing horse, a cowering peasant beneath its feet. Equine depictions are seen throughout the Abbey, most often in the heraldic memorials on the walls of the nave. They depict strength, and in royal plaques are often represented by the most noble horse, the unicorn.

The animals carved in stone here are often native to Britain, including any number of cattle and asses, but some of the most fun ones hail from other shores. Monkeys and lions play significant roles, though it is interesting to note that you seldom get a whole lion. Often, there is just a head, while on the Andrewes family memorial there is a solitary foot, the other one lost in the mists of time. *Lost: One lion's paw. Please return to the left-hand side of Andrewes family memorial, Hexham Abbey, Northumberland* – an appeal for its return might say.

From stone, let's return to wood. I've already mentioned the roof bosses, while below are the medieval choir stalls and misericords. The misericords' name derives from the Latin *misericordia* – have pity. These are tip-up seats that allowed monks from the early 15th century to perch when they were supposed to be standing throughout long services. It was thought unseemly to sit upon religious images, so the carvers were able to opt for pagan imagery, which is to me all the more fun. Animals appear regularly, as do strange beasts including a bearded man whose bottom half is a chicken; a wyvern (with a serpent's body and bat-like wings); and a female satyr (with a human face and, again, bat wings). Finally, our old friend the Green Man makes another appearance.

There are so many beasts here, the Abbey would have had Noah scratching his head as to where to fit everyone in his ark, but before we leave, I enjoyed a modern portrayal of an animal. In the Big Story exhibition in the restored former monastery buildings there is a modern mural depicting life in the medieval period. If you look hard enough, you will see that it is full of cheeky images, my favourite being a little white terrier cocking his leg on a rather smart lady's shoe. It's the sort of thing my old terrier Reg would have taken great pleasure in.

Back in the Abbey, as I headed for the door I was confronted by a splendid carved bench featuring the city of Newcastle's coat of arms. As you might know, this features three castles supported by two seahorses and at the top a lion holding the golden staff of Saint George's pennant. This splendid piece of furniture was made for Queen Victoria to take the weight off her feet during the opening of Newcastle Central Station. I briefly sat on it, as it is not often that I get to share the seat of royalty, and found that it commands a splendid view of the Abbey's magnificent crossing and north transept. Why it is here rather than at the train station it was made for, no-one is entirely sure, but I think Her Majesty might have approved.

My mind now a bestiary of wonderful creatures, I stood and made my way out into the Market Place, as people have done for a very long time, and I hope will continue to do for another 1,350 years.

~

SIX

Stinging
& Prickling

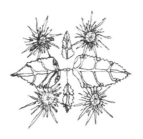

There is a man in Dorset called Clive Farrell. He has been described as the Lord of the Butterflies. When I lived down that way, I had a garden nursery called Monty Watts Plants that specialised in plants for butterflies and bees. Clive was the font of all knowledge about which plants attracted the insects I was after, and he kindly guided me on which species worked best and how I should propagate them.

One of the intriguing things he had on his farm was a plant prison where the thugs of the borders were prevented from spreading by walls with deep foundations. The plants inside had definite benefits to insects, but would not be welcome in a flower border. Two inmates I remember well were thistles and nettles. Thistles are excellent for butterflies as a nectar source, and nettles are a food source for numerous species of butterfly caterpillar. However, in my day-to-day life on the farm, I curse them both.

Nettles and thistles are a grazier's nightmare. They spread quickly and take away the ability of cattle and sheep to graze freely; hence good grazing goes to waste. However, casting my eye over a particularly impenetrable thicket of thistles the other day, I wondered, could these beasties actually be of more use than just keeping our butterfly and bee populations happy?

The answer, I am glad to say, is yes, and

once I started digging into the life and times of nettles and thistles, I found they serve more purposes than you can shake a stick at.

Immersing yourself in the world of plants and their qualities is a complex business. This is mainly because over time you learn that their uses have changed as science has sped along. But I am, as you know, broad-minded, so I'm going to give you the full breadth of the knowledge I have garnered in my potters through the tomes of the Literary & Philosophical Society in Newcastle. However, what you are about to read comes with a strict health warning. Do not imbibe, eat, rub or mess about with any of the plants I am about to mention without proper medical advice. As we all know, one man or woman's tonic is another's poison. You have been warned!

Let's get back to those pesky nettles. Readers of my articles in *The Northumbrian* magazine will remember that they have cropped up before. When I was looking at what the Romans did for us in the magazine and in my first book,

STINGING & PRICKLING

Down the Rabbit Hole, nettles were among the host of horrors the Romans brought to these shores. Their idea of a good time was to thrash themselves with the things to keep out the winter chills when standing about on Hadrian's Wall waiting for the blue-armed army to appear.

Now, the good news is that if you carefully pick young nettles using thick gloves then you have a very nutritious plant. Once boiled, the stings disappear and you can incorporate them into delicious stews and soups. These dishes then give you nettle goodies like iron, vitamin A and vitamin C, which are great for your blood, your immune system, and for ailments like arthritis.

I said I'd give you the full range of the knowledge I have picked up on my meanderings through the Lit & Phil's copious collection of books on British plants. An absolute gem is *A New Herbal* by William Turner. He wrote it in the 16th century in the cloisters of Cambridge, but he was by birth a Morpeth, Northumberland, man, so his local knowledge had to be worth a peek.

He starts quite mildly, recommending nettles for dog bites and nose bleeds. However, it doesn't take William long to get a bit more X-rated. Skip to thistles if you are of faint heart, because according to him, "*the seed drunken with Malvasia stirreth a man to pleasure of the body and openeth the mother.*" I am as red as a nettle sting writing this, but I guess Ann Summers wasn't even a glint in the woodsman's eye in 1551, so you had to get your sex education where you could find it. You'll be glad to know that he goes on: "*The same licked up with honey is good for stopping up the pipes ...*" Which pipes, I have no idea.

Back to the present, and I can't have you wandering about in the nettle patch without giving you some advice should you be stung. Since I was a child, I have soothed nettle stings by rubbing them with crunched up dock leaves. They kind of work, but if you want a really good way to stop the irritation and inflammation, then grab a handful of plantain. Again, crush it in your hands to release the juices and rub on the affected area. You will shortly be skipping along the lane singing a jolly song as if nothing has happened.

Now for some thistles. I came across them early in life. One of my favourite books to have read to me at bedtime was *The House at Pooh Corner*. I'd be amazed if you haven't had this read to you or even read it yourself. My dad had a friend in the SAS who told me that this collection of delightful stories found its way into many a sticky situation as the soldiers loved its ability to transport them away from a fox hole to the delightful world of the Hundred Acre Wood.

You have to agree that Pooh and Piglet often dare and win, and these two rightly get a lot of the limelight. However, I think my favourite character is Eeyore. He leads a rather solitary life in a thistle patch. It doesn't seem to bother him. I get the impression that while munching thistles he is ruminating on larger issues, perhaps, as Bill Bailey put it, "the pearlescent tear in a Peruvian shepherd's eye as he considers his last dawn."

I don't know, but Eeyore is a thistle fan. That bit did cause me some consternation as a child. My first memory of thistles was trying to go paddling in a twinkling stream in the Yorkshire Dales. I cast aside my brown Clark's sandals and stepped forth only to get what felt like 12,000 volts through my foot. It was a thistle in the 'rosette' stage lurking flat to the ground. Leaping in pain, I soon landed on another and another. "Bother . . ." said Charlie.

I shouldn't malign thistles. Our friends north of the border venerate them to such a degree that one forms their national emblem. Why? For the same reason that I was sent skyward by their multiple prickles. Viking warriors trying to creep up on a Scottish redoubt stupidly took off their boots for a stealthy approach. Unfortunately for them it was dark, and the thistles did their business. "Bother . . ." said the Vikings as they were chased back to their longboats. The victorious Scots then had reason to embellish everything from shortbread tins to rugby shirts with the things.

Thistle benefits aren't only for keeping away marauding Vikings, feeding ponderous donkeys, and keeping small boys from their paddling. One species, the milk thistle, has many benefits for your health. If you pop into most pharmacies, you will find it in pill form. Have a chat with the pharmacist, but I understand that it will help your liver function and blood sugar health; it will increase milk production if you are breast-feeding; it will improve acne; and possibly even help to fight against cancer. I don't think it says this on the bottle, but I know from experience that after perhaps a few too many drinks, if you can remember to take some milk thistle pills your hangover will be more manageable.

I can't leave the thistles without seeing what our friend William Turner had to say. You will be pleased to know that this time he keeps us clear of his bedroom antics. However, he does claim that the thistle is good for the biting of serpents. Adders certainly seem to have been more abundant in those days, so it is good to know that a shot of anti-venom was always nearer than Holland & Barrett. He also claims thistles were good for cleaning your teeth (ouch) and soothing toothache, and they would also help you with tummy upsets. As with nettles, he then gets into some plumbing that I don't really understand: "*In a broth it is good for the parts that have bursten and shrunken together.*"

For this story I set off with a list of plants to investigate, but it didn't take long to get lost in the world of nettles and thistles. I'll get onto the joys of belladonna and digitalis another day. What in my field had looked like an impenetrable and painful crop of horrors has in fact turned out to be a fascinating journey into the world of two plants with health benefits that should do you some good, or at least keep your pipes right.

~

SEVEN

A Beginner's Guide to Retirement

To be honest, I probably spend too much time sticking my nose into the business of the creatures on our farm. If you were to ask the current Mrs Bennett about my expeditions beyond the back gate, she'd probably ask you to give her back all the hair she pulled out when I was meant to be at sports day or at home waiting for the BT man who'd promised to call sometime between February and March, when actually I was intently watching a mole hill, on my hands and knees looking for vole arenas, or rootling about in a cow pat with my 'going about' stick.

This is meat and potatoes for a jobbing accidental naturalist, but it's not only animal behaviour that interests me. It is also the doings of my fellow Northumbrians and, believe it or not, even those strange folk who live south of the Tyne and north of Carter Bar. The older ones particularly pique my interest – those on the cusp of retirement or on its nursery slopes, and those who have been retired for years but often appear busier than when they were earning an honest crust.

My appreciation of the retired began as a small boy, when my grandfather taught me to fly fish. His advice was profound, as I discovered one afternoon when I'd whipped the River Nidd into a cappuccino-like froth and ended up crestfallen, with no trout on the bank. He smiled and explained: "Charlie, this is not about catching fish, it's about being by the river, being with me or a good friend, or simply watching the world go by." By some miracle, this advice stuck and I'm still happy as Larry when near a river, burn, stream or beck, with or without a rod.

Another inspiring person well beyond retirement age was a man I knew in Somerset called Theo. I was a struggling nurseryman trying to sell plants for butterflies and bees, and I needed a field to propagate my plants. Theo got wind of this and for the princely sum of £20 a month he let me use one of his paddocks.

We became great friends. He was quite eccentric, and had a bath and a loo in his bedroom (a bachelor, he did what any sensible person would do and placed his conveniences close by his scratcher rather than down a draughty corridor). From him I learnt that if you have an idea, no matter how far-fetched, you should follow it through, as it might just work. My love of Radio 3 comes from him, as it was the soundtrack to all our ramblings. He really deserves his own chapter, he was such an inspiration.

There are many more, and the time has come for me to pay them the compliment of passing on the behaviour I have seen from the successfully retired. This is advice for those staring down the barrels of an uncertain future when work comes to an end, or those who find the Saga ads aren't what they're cracked up to be.

First, you need to be properly attired. You will have favourite old clothes; the ones you don't mind talking to the postman in, or at a stretch, collecting the newspaper. For me, that's an old shirt, preferably with none of the original material around the collar, a V-neck sweater with more holes than wool, old cords with patches that don't match in colour or material, and when heading outside, my Husky. This quilted coat of at least 20 winters looks like one of my old Airfix Spitfires, which had puffs of cotton wool along their flanks to indicate where they had been strafed by Messerschmidts. In my coat, the cotton wool has been caused by skirmishes with brambles, barbed wire, and small terriers. A squashy old cap is a good addition, or even, to use a modern term, a 'beanie' (a woolly hat to you and me). And for the feet I have old sailing shoes called Sebagos that seem to last for ever and look like old burnt pies, but are excellent for most occasions when walking is required.

So, you're suitably clad. Now what to do? The answer is head for the chair – the most comfortable one in the house. This is the first rule of retirement, and this is the place in which you can nod off at any time of the day with no guilt attached.

For maximum snoozage, make sure you're on top of the log situation, the dogs have been walked, and your phone is turned off. And if asked what you've been doing all day, reply: "Training for the Olympic Egyptian PT team." (For the uninitiated, this involves sleeping soundly like an Egyptian pharaoh in a tomb). If pre-PT you are caught by your other half contentedly musing about nothing and asked what you're thinking about, the answer is: "How compatible we are, darling."

Snooze over – now what? Well, you need to be able to extend your ability to cook, the reason being that cooking means shopping for delicious things. It also means making a wonderful mess and the opportunity to employ your full range of expletives. If this stage comes on, you can do another wonderful thing and drink gin.

Once dinner is cooked, you can impress your family and friends and perhaps get invited for a rematch (another thing about retirement – see as many of your old mates as possible). And one final bit of advice in this section: wash up. For this is the balm of rocky marriages, the forgiveness of useless flatmates, and the lubrication of the best group holidays.

Full of food, return to the chair, where you may nod off. Or read a book. Or try to remember all the books you've meant to read in your life but never got around to. Or go back to the ones you loved as a kid, though some don't bear the test of time very well.

I find Wilbur Smith, Patrick O'Brien and Eric Newby are usually good places to start. You will have your own favourites, and if they're not already on your bookshelf, go to your local independent bookshop. There aren't many independent ones left, but what a treat when you do find one. If they don't have *The Mole* by UR Myopic they will order one in. As a start try Barter Books in Alnwick for secondhand books, coffee and cake.

Now it's time to plan things further afield, because you can go on holiday when everyone else is at work or at school, meaning everything is cheaper and less busy. I'd like to go to Montana for the fishing, and also to bring in the herd. I'd also like to visit the 34 remaining Vermeers scattered across glorious cities around the world. Or I'd go up the road to Amble, which has the longest street of independent shops in the North East of England, and in Spurreli's the best ice cream parlour anywhere.

What if you can't be chewed to flex the bus

pass or use up the air miles? Well, you can travel to some places from your armchair thanks to wonderful things like Negroni, French 75, Margarita, and Martini. Yes, a few strong cocktails will soon have your mind travelling to the thoughts you had consigned to the Do Not Disturb area of your imagination.

This is when what I call a hi-fi comes in handy. Equally, you might have an electronic friend called Alexa, or perhaps even a wireless. If so, hopefully by now you might have shared a few cocktails with your other half, some friends, or the plumber. Adequately refreshed by the cocktails, it's time to turn up the sounds and jive, giggle or wobble your way around the sitting room until you think bedtime might be a good idea. Now, having successfully negotiated the perilous route to your bedroom you will be faced by your bed. Try hopping on it when it comes round for the third time, or revert to said chair.

Some final thoughts – join the Literary & Philosophical Society in Newcastle, where you will meet wonderful people and learn amazing things (you will need your medium-smart clothes for this – a jumper without holes, for example). And pick up a pen or pencil. Writing, drawing, even painting can seem daunting, but less so if you join a club, where you will find that other essential for successful retirement – friends.

Creativity is like a muscle. The more you exercise it, the better it gets. I was musing with a fellow writer the other day about what makes us keep putting pen to paper. Who are we doing it for? Are we just on a massive ego trip? These are good questions, but we concluded that the simple answer is that it is just an outlet for thoughts that don't come out in any other way. So let them. For example, I had only a small idea of where this story was going when I started tickling the ivories on a wet evening that otherwise would have been no fun at all.

So, it is the end of day one in retirement. You are replete, you have spoken to the travel agent, and had a chat with the old friend you haven't seen in years and with whom you will now be going to the Lit & Phil. You're quite pleased with the dance moves that didn't squash the dog or break granny's prized vase. Your other half hasn't had so much fun in years, nor seen you so happy.

Now repeat for years to come, adding new activities whenever they come your way. This will keep the mixture lively, interesting and never boring. One last thing: please share your knowledge and new-found passions with the rest of us. We need you now more than ever to keep us entertained until we too skip over the bridge of retirement.

~

EIGHT

Welcome Guests

I t is often said that guests are a bit like fish, the reason being that they both go off after about three days. In the wild it is a bit more of a mixed bag, with guests that are welcome for as long as they want and others who almost immediately overstay their welcome.

My favourite guests are swallows. One day last year, I was standing in the yard wondering where I had put the keys to the tool shed. I seem to have a strange relationship with keys, putting them down in the most unlikely places.

CLIMBING STILES

Recent discoveries by Mrs Bennett have been in the fridge and on the roof of the car as I was driving off. So when I lose them there is lot of back-tracking going on in my mind and righteous concern that I will shortly be on the end of a WIK – Wigging in the Kitchen.

This lovely April morning, my deep ponderings and worries of impending WIKs were disturbed by the throaty chuckle of a swallow, which had just landed on a telegraph wire above my head. I am always in awe at the thought that they come all the way from Africa, so this one sent a shiver down my spine and the keys were forgotten as a tear had come to my eye. Swallows can do that to me – a bit like bagpipes at weddings.

In spring and summer a lot of guests pitch up on the farm. Some, like the swallow, are old friends and can stay as long as they like. Others are unexpected and often as unwelcome as news that the septic tank has breached its bounds.

You may or may not be aware that we are

in the midst of a large biodiversity project – a bout of common-sense farming, as I like to call it. This has involved many new and exciting projects. There is a saying, "build it and they will come". Well, in the case of wildlife it is true. One day, the maestro of pond digging John had finished a particularly pleasing pond. He can make shapes that make the heart sing and, having completed this particular piece of art, he turned off his 18-tonne digger, hopped out for a bit of craic on the ways of the world, and skedaddled.

The pond was already filling with water from a ground spring and I was checking to see where it might potentially leak. Old field drains are a menace to the pondsman or woman and need to be blocked before they empty away any water that might have been thinking of gathering and making a pleasing water feature. But what actually caught my eye was a water boatman. What a treat – the pond was a day old and this perky little critter was already hunting for supper in the gin-clear waters.

The water boatman is an extraordinary creature. The one I spotted had obviously been flying about on the lookout for a spot of supper and once it had plopped in, unbeknown to me it would have started hunting about for algae and plant matter. This one was the small species. If you see its larger cousin, beware, as these are carnivorous, hoovering up tadpoles and even small fish. They are not to be tackled as they can bite and give you a small but painful dose of venom. All species are able to move extremely nimbly through water. They are propelled by long hind legs, which are covered with hairs and used like oars, hence their name. The middle legs are slightly shorter and the front legs shorter still as they are used for scooping up food.

All in all, this is a very efficient aquatic hunter. However, the water boatman's hunting and manoeuvrability are not its star turns. No, this has the honour of being the loudest animal on Earth relative to its body size. Scientists have recorded them "singing" at up to 99.2 decibels, the equivalent of listening to a rock band in the front row. This sound is largely dissipated by water, but it is still audible to humans passing a pond or watercourse where a male water boatman is trying to attract a mate.

How does he make this extraordinary noise? Well, this is one of those biological wonders that honestly makes my eyes water, so if you are faint-hearted, please hop to the next paragraph. You see, the water boatman has a singing penis. Yes, it makes its song by rubbing its penis against its abdomen in a process known as stridulation. This might be why, despite their many attributes, you don't see many water boatmen on *Britain's Got Talent*.

Let us leave the murky depths of the pond and take to the air. Around late May or June, we receive a delightful guest, the painted lady butterfly. It, like our friend the swallow, arrives from Africa, its journey an amazing feat when you consider the distance and numerous perils along the way.

On arrival it is on the lookout for food –

nectar in its case – and a good place to lay its eggs. This is why I like the painted lady, as its arrival means one of our unwelcome guests is about to get its marching orders.

One of the few downsides of letting John loose with his yellow beastie is that you leave a lot of beautifully shaped but bare soil around the ponds. Lurking in this freshly exposed dirt are the seeds of numerous plants itching to come to life with a drop of rain and a bit of summer sunshine. Sadly, a few are not that welcome – nettles and docks come to mind, and thistles are a real pain. They do have their benefits and I am coming to turn a blind eye as they are amazing sources of nectar for numerous insects and in the winter clouds of goldfinches love the seed. However, for the ponds and the trees we plant around them they make maintenance a painful chore.

Luckily, our painted lady comes to our aid. Having supped at the thistle's nectar, the female may well lay her eggs on its stems, its spikes protecting against browsing herbivores which otherwise might inadvertently eat our butterfly's precious eggs. Once the eggs hatch then the caterpillars get stuck into the thistles.

Spotting these caterpillars, I often woop with joy as I then know my neighbours won't be getting a dose of my thistles on the next puff of wind. Once the caterpillars have had their fill they turn into a cocoon and will emerge as fully formed butterflies in August and September. Isn't metamorphosis great? I wish I could hunker down only to appear as something completely different at a later date. Perhaps a key-remembering husband? Sadly, the painted ladies can't survive our winter, so the whole British population either succumbs to winter's icy tendrils or the wise ones emigrate back to Africa, hence why the whole process can start again next year.

I have written at some length in the past about hedges. They are, as you might remember, one of my favourite habitats on the farm. They take different forms. We have our old established hedges that are now into three years of not being cut. These bushy, untidy avenues of loveliness are the hotel that many of our guests flock to, the highlight being 300 yellowhammers I witnessed pouring out one day. However, daily I see a huge array of birds – dunnocks, blackbirds, whitethroats, wrens; the list goes on and on. In the depths of these hedges small mammals proliferate and in the damp corners toads and other invertebrates hunt about for insects and grubs.

However, the old hedges are not our only ones, as we also have new examples. Over the last two years we have planted 10km of them. Like teenagers, they are delightful but have their problems. Deer and hares love eating them, so I march for miles spraying Trico on them. This magical elixir made from sheep's wool is detested by deer and hares so the plants are left to get on with getting big and bushy. However, I am often literally undermined by our long-term diminutive guest the vole. They sharpen the bottom of hedge plant stems like pencils, rather like mini-beavers. The new hedges are surrounded by grasses left to grow as the hedges are fenced against stock. This in turn creates vole heaven as largely they can go about their business under a thatch of old grass. I am delighted to say that our now numerous barn owls are adept at plunging through the grasses to capture our little hedge sharpeners. I love barn owls almost as much as swallows and can spend hours watching them floating up and down the hedgerows.

Lastly, we have unofficial hedges. These are largely areas where the old hawthorns were over-cut in the past and died. What tends to take their place are brambles, and over time they have made impenetrable prickly thickets. Brambles are a delight for many of our summer and indeed autumn guests. They produce numerous flowers that have nectar for a bevy of insects and when they are pollinated produce delicious fruit that is loved by birds, labradors and of course us lot. Meantime, throughout the summer and beyond the roe deer which nomadically browse around the farm will often stop for a nibble on the blackberry leaves.

Our final guest is me. Someone asked me, "how long is your plan for the farm?" They were from a big corporation looking at the farm as a way of making their business sustainable. I asked them to tell me how long their plans were first, as I guessed they would be surprised by my answer. They work largely to five-year plans they said, so they found it hard to comprehend that my plan is for 200 years. I have realised that I need to see beyond my and my children's lifetimes to a time when many of the trees, ponds and hedges will just be coming into their own. So in that time frame I am a bit like another of our summer guests – the mayfly. For them, time is short, but they efficiently manage to get everything done before shuffling off this mortal coil. I hope I will be the same, but where are those keys?

~

NINE

Farm Orbit

Our friends at NASA spend a lot of time and money looking for life in outer space. I have often wondered if this is a good idea, mainly because it might be rather inconvenient if the life they find has run out of resources and needs a new home. ("Where is it you said your planet is?" Ummm . . .).

If you follow NASA's logic, the other populated planets in the universe are probably doing the same thing. And while you might hope our new friends would want to benefit both our civilisations, Earth might also be stripped bare and left for an Elon Musk on another planet to say, "Ooh, look at this place, it's a bit like Mars. There might have been life here once . . ."

I write this on international Earth Day, having been imagining that a NASA message has been received by beings from another world and they have sent a representative to check us out. Of course, the location of their landing would not be America, as in all the films, but Northumberland, in particular this nook where I live, and this story is written from the perspective of an imagined alien visitor. Their mission log, I imagine, would read as follows:

Earth date – April 22 in the year 2024. Mission – Orbit of Greenside Farm. Earthlings in attendance – Bipod Charlie Bennett (human), quadrupeds Ella and Frog (canine):
Having fed chocolate peanuts to the bipod

and toast to the quadrupeds, we conduct our pre-launch briefing. The quadrupeds, who are identified as Ella and Frog, seem to find this boring, but once we set coordinates for the Somme Wood they cheer up and set off enthusiastically sniffing the ground, which makes me feel at home as this is our favourite sport on Planet Tundra.

Soon we reach the edge of the wood; a magical place alive with birdsong and huge queen bumblebees, which like us are looking for new homes. Charlie examines a wildlife camera to see if squirrels ("hopefully red," he says) are in attendance. So far, he has seen everything but.

After a pleasing interlude examining wildflowers and ancient rocks, Charlie takes aim for an open space known as 'the fields'. Then we enter a small plantation. "What is that noise?" I ask Charlie. "That is the sound of bees and other insects feeding on willow flowers," he says.

We come to a slow-moving body of water

known as a stream with a thing called a pond at the end. In the middle of this is what looks like a collection of eyes all looking in different directions. "Frog spawn," Charlie says. "The eggs of amphibians called frogs that start life in water."

I am amazed, as the frog I met previously is huge and hairy. However, Charlie goes on to explain that before they become frogs, these creatures are something called tadpoles, which then become froglets and finally frogs (again, I cannot see the resemblance to the furred canine). Further along the stream, Charlie shows me some tadpoles swimming and apparently sunbathing in a shallow pool.

I still can't see how the hairy quadruped now bounding through the long grass started out so small, but Charlie, like his dogs, has swiftly moved on to study a thing called a feather, which is lying on the surface of another pond. These structures allow Earth animals called birds to fly, I am told. "Mandarin," Charlie says. My knowledge of Earth culture is advanced, and I wonder what an ancient Chinese bigwig has been doing paddling in a pond. Charlie, however, declares: "No, a duck, and ducks are birds that live on or near water." Heavens to Betsy, whatever next?

We are now approaching the outer reaches of another wood. I am startled when a grey bird bursts out of the foliage and disappears over the horizon. "That is a pigeon," Charlie tells me. "They can navigate by seeing north. They have a mineral called magnetite in their beaks that is then connected to their eyes."

"Hmmmm, useful," I say. Charlie looks worried and leads me further into the wood by a wiggly path between the trees.

"Have other bipeds made this?" I ask. "No, deer," says Charlie, perhaps overly affectionately bearing in mind that we have only just met. At this moment we spot three heart-shaped furry white rear ends bounding into the distance. We follow them out of the wood and into the field, where their owners stop, turn to look back at us and then bounce over the horizon.

CLIMBING STILES

Looking down, I notice bright yellow circles everywhere on the field's surface, often with small life forms resting on them. "Dandelions," Charlie says. "An essential source of early nectar for small creatures called insects."

"What is nectar?" I ask.

"Fuel for small things," Charlie says.

This is also of particular interest.

The end of our orbit is in sight, and I hear magical music high in the sky. "Skylarks," says Charlie. "The males are looking for a mate and telling other skylarks where their territory is."

We are in view of mission control and the canines accelerate away as they sense home is close at hand. I am feeling light-headed and short of breath. An alarm sounds in my helmet and a sensor flashes up to tell me that Earth air is toxic for us Tundranites. Charlie is concerned. "Anything I can do?" he asks. "Just get me to my craft and I'll be on my way," I say.

So Charlie carries me to my machine and gently puts me in the driving seat. "Goodbye," he says, "lovely to meet you."

FARM ORBIT

"You are a lucky bipod," I croak. "This is a beautiful place."

"I know," says Frog the dog, as Charlie closes the door.

I press the 'Home' button and watch with a tear in my eye as this beautiful blue planet gradually shrinks and fades in the rear-view mirror.

~

TEN

Turned Out Nice Again

“Turned out nice again . . .” is an ironic refrain I associate particularly with planting trees last year in horizontal sleet. Our ability to make light of the weather is a core survival skill in this country, surrounded as we are by often perilous seas that bring with them a cornucopia of weather from every point of the compass. And this ever-changing mixture of forecasts can have a big impact on our lives.

In the countryside, the weather directly affects our livelihoods. A couple of years ago, for example, saw some of the hottest days on record and on the hottest of all, a scorching 39C, we decided to make hay. It was perfect – the grass cut like butter, and like a ready-made chicken tikka out of the microwave, was instantly ready for action (that is, baling). All went to plan – the baler tore along, giving birth to huge square bales every few minutes, and shortly the tractor and baler were gone, leaving behind peaceful, freshly mown fields where the swallows were free to swoop like Spitfires to pick up the insects disturbed by the kerfuffle.

But very hot days like this are a double-edged sword. They make hay-making possible, but they often have a sting in the tail in the form of a thunderstorm. Thus, bang on cue, as the baler left, huge cumulus nimbus started to form in the west.

Do you remember TV's *Thunderbirds*? I wish I'd had the number for International Rescue, but in its absence I desperately hit the phone looking for help. Fortunately, as ever in our neck of the woods, a neighbour came to my aid, and with the help of my son we had the field cleared before the real deluge began.

On an evening like that with no hay to be made, I would have been in an even more optimistic frame of mind. This is because a hot day followed by a warm, heavy evening is the perfect combination for trouting. Scientists quibble over whether or not fish react to barometric pressure, but I have no doubt, which means that when it's warm and thunder is on the way I will be heading hot-foot to the riverbank. If you get it right, the wild brown trout will be rising at a ferocious rate, the surface of the water popping like a glass of Champagne.

The Wansbeck trout is a wily beast and a badly presented fly will spook it, which means you won't be rewarded with a tasty supper. I have learnt that a fly called a Grey Wulff, gently cast about 9ft upstream to a rising fish, will often do the trick, though if the fish takes you

have to strike quicker than lightning to keep
a hold of it. Lightly fried in butter and served
with new potatoes and salad, this is the food of
the gods.

While we're in foraging mood, the weather
always plays a part in what we find around the
farm. Remember Storm Arwen in November
2021? For one night it was like living in a
washing machine, except rather than a storm of
socks, we were battered with trees, sheds, roof
tiles and goodness knows what else.

But every cloud has a silver lining. Yes, we
had a lot of trees down, and this was sad as
some were venerable old friends two centuries'
old, including my favourite oak. But we set
to clearing timber, bringing it to the yard,
chopping it into logs, and most satisfying of
all, stacking them. I'm a bit of a log librarian
(or bore, some might say) and I have separate
bays for different vintages. Usually, the longer
you can season logs, the better they get. That
year was unusual, as the logs split in November
2021 had already seasoned by November 2022,

the reason being that crazy hot summer I mentioned earlier.

This surfeit of logs has been a godsend not just for me, but for the wider population of Northumberland. Kate Thick's charity, Northumberland Log Bank, got busy gathering logs from farms and estates across the county, to be distributed to more than 400 fuel-impoverished folk. If anyone deserves an MBE, it is Kate, who is the founding trustee of the charity.

So, we might be sitting by the log burner with the rain lashing down outside. In our house this doesn't always mean a warm glow of smugness, however, because our old farmhouse is like a sieve. If the rain comes from the east, the place starts leaking, resulting in a mad charge for buckets and the removal of rugs and aged relatives. While this warming activity is in full flow, I might be bowled over by our labrador Ella looking for a hiding place as a crack of thunder explodes overhead and for a second the valley is lit by a fork of lightning.

But this presents another silver-lined cloud through the maelstrom. You see, lightning is great news. With up to 1 billion volts of electricity, lightning burns at 50,000 degrees, making it hotter than the surface of the sun. When lightning strikes, it tears apart the bond in airborne nitrogen molecules. Those free nitrogen atoms then have the chance to combine with oxygen molecules to form a compound called nitrates. Once formed, the nitrates are carried down to the ground by rainfall. There, plants can absorb the powerful natural fertiliser.

This is great news for newly sewn meadows, freshly planted hedges, and woods. The rain that comes with it also freshens our ponds. So once the buckets are in place and the thunder has passed, we can sit in front of the telly. Unless the wind has taken down the power lines, that is.

We come at last to my favourite weather – snow. Yes, I know it can be a pain. During the Beast from the East in 2018 (remember that?)

we were snowed in for three days with no power, and it was a weird feeling, knowing that we had no access to the outside world. But at the same time it was a proper adventure, and we built snowmen, cooked on the log burner and read by Tilley lamps.

Friends hiked through the snow to bring that essential ingredient for survival – gin. This made escorting them home more interesting than the usual wander over the fields, as the combination of deep snowdrifts and huge hilarity hampered our progress. I guess this is one of those 'don't do this at home' things (with apologies to our local Mountain Rescue).

Snow does offer the opportunity of fun, but it is what it does to the landscape that I really love. We live in a beautiful place and with a thick covering of snow it takes on a new dimension. It is almost timeless, the valleys and woods looking like they might have done hundreds of years ago. If you're really lucky, this is combined with sun and a bright blue sky, and a walk is a treat, the snow issuing pleasing deep sighs with every step.

It's important to keep your eyes peeled on days like this. For it may well have been snowing through the night, but this doesn't mean nature has been idle, and you'll quickly start picking up the tracks of rabbits and deer. You might also see the clues of nocturnal drama. I have written before about when our local wildlife expert George Dodds showed me marks in the snow that showed a lucky vole had escaped the attentions of a barn owl.

I was listening to a song the other day called *Change* by Big Thief. It asks some good questions, including: *Would you live forever, never die? Would you smile forever, never cry? Would you stare forever at the sun, never watch the moon rising? Would you walk forever in the light to never know the secret of the quiet night?* I might add to that, would you always have lovely days? I wouldn't, because then you might miss those silver linings.

~

ELEVEN

Under
the Thatch

W e were recently carrying out a survey on the farm to see if we have harvest mice. There are pockets of these delightful creatures across Northumberland and word had got around that our farm, with its plentiful wild grassy areas, might be a perfect home.

As we hunted, we came across endless runs and creatures scurrying away ahead of us. Harvest mice? Sadly not – these were the participants of a vole plague.

This is not a bad thing: the field voles who are running amok across our farm are very welcome visitors. The chief surveyor piqued my interest when she showed me a vole arena. Yes, a vole arena … Not a mini-amphitheatre with a diminutive Russell Crowe at the centre screaming: "Are you not entertained?" This was actually a small clearing about 10cm in diameter with a roof made of grass thatch. If you weren't looking, you would never know it existed.

In this arena the vole sits and chews on its main foodstuff – grass. Tiny remnants of grass stems were in evidence, and neatly piled in one corner the result of that diet – tiny egg-shaped poos of iridescent green.

In the UK, there are estimated to be 75 million voles, which is quite a lot of poo when you think about it, and that means the voles are doing a grand job of improving our soils. I was hooked and determined to find out more about the field vole, so off I set to my favourite place in the world, The Literary & Philosophical Society in Newcastle.

I've written before about this treasure trove of books, music and manuscripts; a happy hunting ground for my research into the human, farming and natural history of our farm. Once again, I wasn't disappointed. The two main rooms are wonderfully old, the floor space filled with oak bookshelves reaching up like mini– Marble Arches to about 15ft above you.

Scattered among these are marble busts of local worthies like my hero Thomas Bewick, and perched on top of the bookcases are surprises including a stuffed baboon. The walls are book-lined on two levels, reaching up to domed ceilings with beautiful circular ceiling lights allowing in natural light. The second levels are reached via tight, vertigo-inducing iron spiral staircases, and narrow balconies give you access to yet more books.

To the uninitiated, it is a labyrinth of books with similar topics dotted around but not

together, often due to their time of publication.
You need a guide to it all, and fortunately the
place is home to Newcastle's population of
polymaths. They don't work there but seem
to live there, expanding their knowledge of
anything and everything. Being the kind-
hearted people they are, they are willing to
share the whereabouts of the treasures on the
shelves; you only have to ask.

It wasn't long before, Alice-like, I was chasing
a wise white-haired rabbit around the shelves.
He was perplexed: we found books on the mole,
the badger and the otter, but not one dedicated
to the vole. A little more burrowing and an
excellent source was found, *Mammals in The
British Isles* by L Harrison-Matthews.

Not long after all this excitement at the Lit
& Phil (I lead a quiet life), I was confronted by
a dead vole lying on the side of a track running
through one of the hay fields. How was I able
to identify the deceased? I had already dug
into L H-M's lovely book. Field voles are small,
weighing 20g-40g (to give you an idea, three

2p pieces weigh about 20g). They have greyish-brown fur, small ears and a short tail. They live mainly in grassland, scrub and dense cover. They make runways and build nests under the thick mat of grass above and around them. They are found across the British Isles but not in Ireland, the Isle of Man, Orkney or Shetland. It is thought they were probably accidentally introduced a very long time ago. Their diet is almost completely made up of grass stems. This means they can live in a relatively small area, as they usually have an abundance of grass around them.

They are prolific in the business of breeding. A female can have three to six litters a year with up to seven pups in each. So you can imagine that with the right amount of grass and a lack of predators, it doesn't take long for the population to explode. Those pups I was telling you about are weaned after a couple of weeks and not long after that are themselves ready to mate. They live for about a year so have to get busy. Quite a thought: a human year for a dog is seven years;

for a vole it is 80.

You might have noticed that I said the deceased. Well, this is a bit of a murder mystery. PC Bellweather's report might read: "On the morning of the 20th February Mr Bennett found Mrs Vole (deceased) on the side of a track in the East Pasture. The post-mortem discovered no visible cause of death."

Initially, I was thinking that I might need a Poirot or Miss Marple to gather the suspects in the piano room at the Lit & Phil and lead us to the murderer. It wasn't a mad thought. Our plague of voles has attracted a Cluedo of suspects: owls, sparrowhawks, buzzards, kestrels, foxes, stoats and weasels. You can imagine them sitting around nonchalantly in the carriage in *Murder On The Orient Express*, knowing that there wasn't one murderer but that they all might have had a hand in the demise of Countess Voleinski.

However, the "leetle grey cells" of Hercule Poirot won't be bothered by my vole's untimely end. The main reason for vole deaths when they are in plague proportions is stress. They build up into such huge numbers that they start encroaching on each other's territories. This means the females spend a disproportionate amount of time defending their territory rather than looking after their young. Eventually, this psychological effect becomes physical, and they lose the ability to breed. Along the way many succumb to stress, as in my example.

This is not unlike when Europeans pitched up in countries where people were living perfectly happy lives without any extra humans, thank you. The settlers then caused the usual mayhem with disease, war and lots of extra people. Many ancient peoples just gave up the will to live and stopped reproducing.

When the voles reach this unhappy point their demise is swift and the population quickly crashes. This has a huge knock-on effect on our usual suspects. A once-ready food source disappears overnight, and they too will see their own populations fall.

The good news is that a small population

of voles will survive and the whole process will start again. You might even witness this. As the breeding season ramps up from March to October, the males produce an unpleasant musky smell and when defending their territory emit loud squeaks. Aren't they lucky that Mrs Vole finds Mr Angry and Mr Smelly irresistible?

So, a quest to find harvest mice has become another rabbit hole I have happily fallen down. What a splendid creature the field vole is, quietly going about its important business in the fields. The next time I spot one in its arena I will tell it: "Yes, I am entertained."

~

TWELVE

The Pancake Inn

This year, a new tool came into my life which has profoundly improved my knowledge of the birds on the farm. It is an app called Merlin, and when you're wandering about gardens, streets, or the countryside it detects the species of birds around you. It is also intuitive and easy to use, even for a Luddite like me.

Birds are largely territorial and with this app you quickly learn that, for example, a series of whistles and snaps and pops aren't three

birds, but a single sedge warbler. Dog walks
that used to take 45 minutes now take hours,
which is good for dogs and not good for getting
to meetings or the school run on time, and
this amazing free technology has dramatically
changed my understanding of the birds on
our farm.

Another group of animals which play an
equally important role in determining how
the environment ticks are farm animals. Plus,
you don't need an app to spot them, as what
you have just trodden in is usually a fairly
good pointer.

I have a deep affection for farm stock. I
think the reason lies in my family history. I was
once asked about my Welsh heritage (though
it wasn't put that politely, but I don't want you
spilling your tea . . .). My new acquaintance
had found out that I was called Bennett and
concluded that I must be Welsh (we were
watching the rugby in a pub in England, so
you can guess who was playing who). Anyway,
having extricated myself more or less in

one piece from this conversation, I was left wondering – could I be Welsh after all?

I phoned my all-knowing aunt and was put in the picture pretty quickly that my great-grandfather had indeed come to Leeds from Swansea. As you know, I am a sucker for a rabbit hole, so into one called www.ancestry.co.uk I dived. After two days of pounding the keyboard, I traced my Welsh ancestors back to 1527, when Nicholas Bennett moved from Derbyshire to Wales to farm the lands of the Earl of Dudley, who was a favourite of Elizabeth I.

That told me I had hundreds of years of family history in Wales, but that I wasn't necessarily Welsh, though I now have a deeper affinity for that amazing country. I also now know that farming has been in my blood for a very long time. Combine that with my mother's side of the family, who are also a long line of farmers, and bingo, you have farm stock hard-wired into your DNA.

I think farming in general gets a hard press

about its effect on the countryside. A lot of that comes from the aftermath of World War Two, when farmers were put upon to produce more food with little regard for the consequences. At the same time, machinery was developing in leaps and bounds and new wonder chemicals were popping up left, right and centre in a perfect storm for the environment. But the farmers were doing as they were told and made a very good job of it. I feel for them, as suddenly their world has turned on a sixpence and now, as if by magic, you have to farm for the environment.

That's easier for me as it's my thing, but not so easy for other farmers who have invested time, money, and generations in getting their farms to produce food for us and keep bread on their own tables. To their credit, they are quickly learning new practices and I am optimistic about the future of farming and the environment.

So, what are farm stock doing for the environment? Well, to answer that question we might focus on the thing you trod in that indicated a cow was in the neighbourhood. That's cow poo, or to use a more charming description, the Cow Dung Community. A cow pat and indeed a sheep's dottle is home to a lively, integrated collection of organisms that have a profound effect on a myriad of wildlife. Or, to use our local wildlife expert George Dodd's description – a place going from soil to song.

Cattle can digest cellulose because they have bacteria called ruminococcus in their rumen. These bacteria produce an enzyme called cellulase that can break down cellulose to glucose which in turn can be used to create energy for the cow. This process is not 100% efficient and when the cow ejects what it can no longer digest the resulting pat is full of a host of nutrients for our dung community. Like any village, a dung community is made up of different characters doing various jobs; the result of their labour being that the dung enriches the soil and allows a plethora of creatures to feed, breed and multiply.

So let's have a look at a few of the characters we might meet at the bar of The Pancake Inn. Take the shiny, portly gentleman and his wife at the bar. That's Sid and Marjorie Dung-Beetle, and they've just had a family of a few thousand little Dung-Beetles. Their type of beetle lay their eggs in dung and once they hatch, the larvae crack on with eating the poo. Their cousins have other ways of spreading their prodigy – some burrowing below a cow pat and pulling the dung into chambers, some rolling it into holes – but the end result is the same; nutritious dung transferred from the surface and into the soil.

Meanwhile, the legless fellow in the snug is Mr Wyatt Worm. He's also had a busy day, he and three of his relations having been busy eating the dung and dragging it down into the soil, which is again the beneficiary.

But not all those propping up the bar are dung eaters. The brown flies playing darts, which are often seen crawling on the surface of a pat laying their eggs, are in fact predators eating smaller flies. In fact, the dung pile is a regular Serengeti of hunters and prey. For example, the phoretic mites which catch a ride on Mr and Mrs Dung-Beetle are on the look-out for fly eggs. This is a symbiotic relationship as fewer fly eggs means fewer grubs eating the dung beetles' breakfast, so the two species rub along just fine.

Lounging by the fire is Roberta Rove-Beetle. She is a streamlined hunter doing as her name suggests – roving the dung pile in search of prey. She has a broad palate and will have a go at mites, beetle larvae, aphids, and small caterpillars both in adult and larvae form.

If I were to describe all the residents of any small human community, I'd need quite a hefty volume, and one pile of dung in a field is equally well-populated. I will list a few more residents to give you the complete picture, and if you'd like to learn more you can pop into the Literary & Philosophical Society in Newcastle and request CVs on them all. They include nematodes, slugs, woodlice, centipedes, millipedes, springtails, harvestmen, spiders, mites, earwigs, and parasitic wasps.

This cornucopia of life doesn't go unnoticed by larger residents on the farm. Crows will flip the piles of dung (perhaps that is why these offerings are called pancakes . . ?) and small birds like wagtails will pounce on flies gathering around a fresh deposit. Meanwhile, larger mammals like badgers will have a rootle for worms.

It's easy to make the mistake of looking at the wild areas on a farm as places where nature abounds. It does, but that is not the complete picture. By combining wild habitats with productive pasture, we can promote a wildlife knees-up only ever seen in places like the bar at The Pancake Inn. Cheers . . . mine's a large one.

~

THIRTEEN

Driven Wild

Driving is one of life's great pleasures. It can be a time of wonderful relaxation, pootling along with the radio tuned into your favourite music, your mind wandering about the delights that lie ahead of you. It can also be a trial if you are caught in traffic with a swarm of screaming kids in the back, and it's not only small children that can make a drive into more of an experience than you had bargained for.

I'll start you off gently in this story of the joys

of driving with wildlife. Coming off a motorway at some speed, I stopped at a red traffic light. I'm telling you about the speed as what I noticed next surprised me. Out of my window I could see a fly suspended in the middle of my wing mirror, this miracle the result of the fly's demise in a spider's web. Despite the gale-force winds that had been whipping around the mirror, the web was still perfectly formed, and as the engine idled and I waited for the lights to change, the owner of the web appeared at a leisurely pace, wrapped up the fly, and took it to its lair behind the mirror.

Spiders are resourceful creatures. Insects, particularly in summer, often come into contact with cars, but how this one thought the wing mirror would be a good idea I don't know. It obviously wasn't self-conscious, as the whole web-building process would have been completed with its reflection bouncing back at it. As you know, I am slightly in awe of these creatures, from the monster which lives in my bath to the one that bit me in the garage, and now I have one of the motoring variety to add to the list.

So, we are gently getting into the idea that wildlife can hitch a ride with you as you make your way about in your car. For the moment we will stick with benign(ish) travellers. During lockdown, my car lay abandoned as I had nowhere to go. By the end of the pandemic my recruitment business had migrated from Newcastle to our house in Northumberland, so the poor old car had to go. I thought I'd look it over before selling it, and lifting the bonnet I was surprised to be met with a storm of little bits of foam. What had caused it? I'll tell you – mice. Having found this sheltered spot full of good nesting spots, they had moved in. What to insulate their nests with and what to nibble on a balmy summer's evening? Oh yes, all that insulation around the wires, tubes and thingummy jobs. The garageist wasn't too surprised. Covid had been bad for cars, but a treat for mice and mechanics.

My friend John had a problem with his new

BMW. He had had it only a short time when he noticed that someone else had been nibbling his mints. Bits of the car's fine trim were also definitely gnawed, and hunting about he found a small hole below the driver's seat. His hunch was that it was mice. He set traps and by the next morning he had caught three. Job done, he thought.

His work then took him on a nationwide motoring odyssey, and I came across him in a frozen pub car park in Gloucestershire. He is normally affable and easy-going, but when I saw him, he was not himself. Motoring down the M5, he had noticed movement out of the corner of his eye. He pretended he hadn't seen it, but then it happened again. Scampering about the leather upholstery was a mouse, and then another, which must be disconcerting when motoring at speed. What, after all, would happen if they decided to scamper on him?

He pulled into a DIY store and acquired the most expensive electronic mouse traps money could buy. When I met him, he had caught another three. He then took the car back. The red-faced salesman eventually got to the bottom of the infestation. New cars had been stored, quietly awaiting new buyers, over the pandemic, and like my rodents and the opportunistic spider, the mice had taken up residence.

Years ago, I had a girlfriend with a rather eccentric mother. On my first visit to the house, I was shown into the sitting room and was moderately alarmed to find, warming itself by the fire, a pig. Not a micro-pig, but a full-scale pink adult. It acknowledged me with a look, closed its eyes and went back to sleep.

I went to the kitchen to inform the mother, Helen, that a somnolent pig had broken in, and discovered her doing a thing you seldom see these days. She had hitched up the back of her skirt, opened the top door of the Aga, and was gently warming her posterior. This she continued as she enquired how I was. I replied that I was well, but there was a pig by her fire. She smiled and called (in a voice that would have been of use to lonely lighthouse

keepers to warn shipping of impending doom)
"Noraaaah!" at which the sound of trotters
could be heard and the pig swanned into the
kitchen to sit dog-like next to her mistress by
the Aga.

On another occasion, Helen decided it was
time the nanny goat, Mary, was mated. I was
informed that Mary needed transporting for
her tryst with a famous billy in Huddersfield,
and using my initiative, I went and attached
the old Rice horse trailer to the equally old blue
and cream Land Rover and drove both around
to the front door to await further instructions.
These weren't long coming. "We don't need
all that," declared Helen. "Put down the back
seats in the VW Golf, fill it with newspaper and
cabbage leaves, and we'll be off."

I'm not sure how many journeys you have
shared with a goat? Well, Mary was an amiable
travelling companion. She spent her time eating
cabbage leaves and putting her head out of the
window and I'm sure that if she could have
spoken, she would have commented on the

delightful blue of the flax fields as they sped by. Instead, however, the cabbages started to do what cabbages do and the car became engulfed in the stink of goat fart. Helen, oblivious, motored on, while I went green.

On arrival, Mary skipped out of the back of the car and went to meet her amour. Unfortunately, this business didn't take long and to my horror I was soon back in the love taxi and its hideous odours. Never again.

A friend once had a similar stinky problem. Driving along a lane one summer's evening, he saw something furry on the side of the road. At the time this friend was not averse to a bit of taxidermy, and often found interesting subjects that had met their demise on the roads. On closer inspection, this was quite a find. It was a weasel that had apparently just caught a rabbit and had probably been crossing the road to take its prey to its den when it was taken out by a speeding jalopy. Weasels are amazing little mustelids (otters, stoats, badgers, to name a few others). They weigh about an ounce, or

25 grams, which compared to the 1kg-2.5kg rabbits they haul about is extraordinary. They catch rabbits by hypnotising them and then striking when their victim has fallen under their spell. Look it up on YouTube – it's an amazing bit of animal behaviour. They then ferry the bunny to share it with their hungry kits.

So, my friend picked up the rabbit with the weasel attached and put them both in his car boot. When he got home, he opened the boot, to be confronted with only the rabbit and a very serious pong. The weasel, it appeared, wasn't dead, just stunned, and in regaining consciousness it had taken fright and let rip (weasels and stouts have scent glands that when activated can strip paint). So, my friend now had two problems. Firstly, where was the weasel? After a lot of hunting about, a gingery flash caught his eye – the weasel exiting the car and making its way to pastures new. As for the hideous smell it had left behind, that took a couple of years to clear, and my friend's love of taxidermy was somewhat diminished.

CLIMBING STILES

We will end with the most dangerous wild
passenger I have come across. One evening
we had a rather jolly time in our fishing hut.
I was driven home by a friend (he was off the
sauce at the time), but it turned out he hadn't
only driven me home, but also a stowaway.
On leaving the hut, I had heard a large wasp
buzzing around my head. This was unusual as
it was 1am, and it had I think been in the cosy
hut with us minding its own business until we
opened the door and it decided to exit with us.
What I didn't know was that the wasp didn't like
the chill of the evening and had decided to seek
some warmth down the back of my jumper.

Duly dropped off at home, I wished my
driver goodnight and headed into the house,
which is when the wasp got a bit uppity.
Whether it was me taking my coat off or
what, I don't know, but it started to sting me
with merry abandon, and I rapidly went from
pleasantly befuddled to full fight and flight
mode. With every expletive I knew I started to
strip until I was naked and I'm afraid it was not

a happy ending for the wasp when I found it. Mrs Bennett observed the whole performance from the top of the stairs and ever since she has loved telling her friends the tale of the small naked man dancing in the hall to the four-letter word song.

So, there you have it. Next time you decide to go for a nice run out in the car, have a look under the seats and behind them, for you never know what might be coming along for the ride.

~

FOURTEEN

Tick, Tock
or Tock, Tick?

Do you know where our obsession with time comes from? Surely, we managed perfectly well before clocks existed. (Caveman One: *"When is the sabre-toothed tiger hunt?"* Caveman Two: *"After breakfast."* See? No clock needed).

Completely by accident, I think I recently discovered where the beginning of time as we understand it comes from. We all know that the best place in the world for finding out about mysterious things is the Literary & Philosophical Society in Newcastle, or more precisely from the hygge of polymaths who live there. But there is a close-ish second in the shape of the British Museum in London. In this woke world it's about as popular as a wasp hiding in your jam sandwich, but I think it is a magnificent place and you should visit it if you are ever at a loose end in the Metropolis. If for only one good reason: on the first floor they have a wonderful collection of clocks.

My usual plan of attack in art galleries and museums is to look at one or two objects and leave savouring the moment (as opposed to getting object blindness). Well, I had gone to look at the ships' chronometers, as I am fascinated about how time allowed sailors to navigate accurately for the first time in 1759. This came about with the wonderful clocks of John Harrison that meant longitude could at last be measured.

There were a few folk hovering over the

chronometers, so I went to look at the case opposite. This was dedicated to the beginning of time-keeping and what caught my eye was a rather lovely gold beaker. It was thinner at the bottom than at the top, rather like a blunt funnel, and it stood about 6 inches high. The bottom was about an inch in diameter and the top had a diameter of about 2½ inches. Peering into the bottom I could see a rod poking up from the middle. It was a bit bigger than a matchstick. Engraved around the inside of the cup were Egyptian numerals.

Below was a card explaining what this object was. Apparently, it belonged to a Time Finder from Ancient Egypt and was a portable sundial. With some deft footwork and a bit of leaning in the right direction, the Time Finder could tell the time of day.

Stop the front page, hold your horses and switch off your mobile phone – this was all news to me. The Time Finder? That must be the coolest job title ever. Jobs like Black Rod, Silver Stick, and Head Keeper of Penguins are all pretty amazing, but the Time Finder? I was immediately thinking Tardis, alchemists, and Lords of the Universe. What a role!

"I *thought, Cleo, we might have the garden fête at 2pm.*"
"*Oh really, Anthony? You know I have a Zoom meeting with Julius then.*"
"*Can you speak to Tut and ask him what the time is?*"
"*It's 4pm, madam.*"
"*Blast, can you come back tomorrow?*"
"*Sorry love, I'm up at Thebes quoting on a job for the pyramid opening.*"

Seriously, what did they need to know the time for? I'm guessing that because sun worship was quite popular, one thing led to another. Chuck in a bit of astronomy and the fact that they were always needing to align buildings with what time it was at particular times of year, then our friend the Time Finder and I imagine his colleagues would have been in constant demand. So the rot started and in only a few millennia the clocks we know today were calling the tune of our daily lives.

My own obsession with clocks started as a smallish boy. My dad had a glazing business that, as well as making bullet-proof glass, glazed the modern (and often, shall we say, interesting) buildings of the 1970s. As a train buff, I know that Peterborough station was once a magnificent place. You only have to look at The Great Northern Hotel. Sitting gracefully across the road from the brutalist, Lego-like booking hall it doesn't take long to realise what a lovely place it must have been to start your journey in one of the magnificent teak coaches of an express train pulled by The Mallard or The Flying Scotsman.

To my now eternal regret, my dad was part of the team that pulled it all down and built the glass and aluminium edifice that largely still stands there to this day. As the place was pulled apart, a lot of the railwayana (yes, that is a word) went into the skip. This included a lovely old clock that had hung proudly in the waiting room. For generations it had reassured passengers that they were still on time for the 2.30pm to York. My beady-eyed dad spotted it and fished it out of its dusty grave and I think gave it to me (or, being the magpie I am, I might have done a clock grab). Anyway, it now sits on the wall in our hall. It has a baritone "tick-pause-tock" soundtrack that I don't really notice until it stops. Then time literally stands still.

The clock has a mind of its own and although I wind it on the same day at the same time, its last tock or tick is when it feels like it. I admire this. I am not a huge fan of today's obsession with time. Have you heard of a ghastly invention called Outlook? It's a calendar on your computer joined at the hip to your email. If you're not careful, your precious time gets stolen by boring meetings, often in that strange ether known as Teams, another kin of the Outlook monster and its hungry calendar. I like a world where time is a bit vaguer; a little less hard to pin down.

CLIMBING STILES

Let me give you an example. Have you ever
been for a 'quick' drink? I can tell you this
concept is as rare as on-time BT engineers, high
street banks, and tasteful holding music. "I'm
going for a quick drink, darling," means that
I go to meet you in the pub, I buy you a pint,
and you, as you are a good person, buy me one
back. Then Bill pitches up. "Pint anyone?" (Er,
um – wondering whether dinner will be in the
oven or the dog . . .) "Oh, okay then." To be
followed by, "Can I get you one, Bill?"

Or you put a baked potato in the oven. These
bullet-like vegetables take about nine years
to cook, unless you pop into the garden to
get some mangetout. Once in the garden you
spot some weeds, then you see the roses need
pruning, so you go to the tool shed to get the
secateurs where you find the half-finished chair
you were mending. "Oh, the potato . . . " you
remember, and return to the kitchen to discover
you have made coal. I have written before
about alchemy, but turning base vegetables into
carbon is not a profitable operation.

TICK, TOCK OR TOCK, TICK?

Time has sped along, leaving you in its wake.
Conversely, it can move very slowly. I was once
in a meeting where my chairman had invited
some monumental bore to lecture us on the
inside of a pencil sharpener or something
equally riveting. As our speaker warmed up, so
did the room, as no windows were open, then
the lights were dimmed for some fascinating
slides. Time became like glue. When would this
ever end, I wondered. I then took the route that
is often open to escape time-lapse moments;
I fell asleep. I was awoken by the lights going
up and my chairman asking, "Any questions
Charlie?" Erm . . .

Have I taken up too much of your time
already? Well, just a tick or hold on a minute
for a brief foray into the wild side of time. Can
animals tell the time? I know dogs can. I could,
I suppose, look into the lineage of my dogs
to find out why. About as much as I know is
that one of our labradors Frog, for example,
is a Drake's Head. No, I don't get it either, but
if we really investigated her genetic makeup,

it would have *Rolex* stamped all over it. She wakes at precisely 8am and starts howling. She is then put out for a wee. She then demands a walk. At precisely 9am she demands breakfast, another walk at 12noon, one at 4pm, then tea at 5pm. She then expects to go for a final wee at 10pm before bed. Exhausting I know, but if coincidentally the hall clock has decided to stop then at least I have my Time Finder.

~

FIFTEEN

Fox, Foxy or Out-foxed?

I suspect it is reasonable to assume that, if you're like me, funerals are not your favourite cup of tea. I certainly don't leap out of bed bright-eyed and bushy-tailed on these occasions, which for some reason seem generally to take place in ghastly crems on dank, drizzly mornings.

I don't understand how we have come to accept crematoria (most of them, at least – there are notable exceptions) as suitable places of departure. Most bring to mind the miserably utilitarian bus stations I remember as a child in the 1970s, which were at their best as they retreated in the driver's rear-view mirror.

Having said that, I have on occasion been fortunate to attend a funeral where the setting was worthy, the most recent being on a sunny day at Hartburn parish church. If you don't know this old Templars' place of worship, then you should visit it, as it is one of Northumberland's finest.

Having completed a moving service, the vicar led us out into the beautiful old churchyard to put a favourite aunt to rest in a fitting setting. This was a perfect day, satisfyingly chilly with not a cloud in the sky. In my memory, a robin might have been singing in a holly bush, but otherwise it was silent. Then, as we gathered for the denouement, my attention was caught by a movement beyond the graveyard wall. The church is on the edge of a dene below which flows the River Hart.

FOX, FOXY, OR OUT-FOXED?

Studying the landscape, I realised that, on the other side of the dene amongst the bracken, a fox was sitting watching us, its head cocked to one side, as a dog's head often is when the animal is engaged in something that piques its interest. Illuminated by the low sun setting off the russet red of its coat, the fox watched the proceedings intently and, as the last words were spoken, moved off gently.

I had a tear in my eye and a lump in my throat. Not only for the late aunt, but for the connection I felt with the fox, and in some strange way for the deep understanding I felt I had subconsciously observed between the fox and the departed.

Am I being over-sentimental, or fanciful, about a fox? Some will say so, but I think not. For humans have been connected to foxes in one way or another for millennia, existing in tandem on every continent apart from Antarctica, and our link is strong.

Foxes do, however, have a bad habit that is not good for their wellbeing, or indeed for ours, in that they like to steal our lunch, and sometimes our livelihoods. We humans like to keep our livestock close at hand where we believe they are safe, but this corralling of sheep, poultry and game presents a fox version of McDonald's which requires constant protection. Thus, you might think that people who have to contend with these highly intelligent predators would hold them in lower esteem than rats or Parisian bed bugs, yet Mr Fox is often highly respected.

The reason for this becomes apparent when we look into their lives in a little more detail. The name fox comes from the old English meaning *thick-haired tail*. Its intriguing Latin name *vulpes vulpes* just means fox (funnily enough, not two foxes), while the other words associated with it are generally rather lovely. *Vixen*, for example, is another old English word (when 'f' was transposed by 'v'), while the fox collective noun is, rather wonderfully, a *leash* or a *skulk*.

Foxes are beautiful, with a flattened skull,

upright triangular ears, a pointed, slightly upright snout, and of course a bushy tail, or brush. Around the world they vary in colour, but in the UK the fox is usually russet red with a white tip on its tail.

They weigh 5kg-8kg and grow to about 40cm at the shoulder. Unlike domestic dogs, they are not long-lived, few progressing much past three years of age. In terms of diet, they are best described as opportunistic omnivores. "*On ze menu zis evening Monsieur Reynard, is a berd, a medley of beetles, wabbits, wats, a veeld vole, a fawn and, for pooding, a brace ov verms . . .*"

Foxes mate in winter, as signified by those eerie screeches from the woods that seem to grace every Agatha Christie film (even when the murder has taken place in mid-summer). A few weeks after the fox and vixen have made sweet music, a litter of four or five cubs will be born. Both parents will take responsibility for feeding their offspring, and may be joined in this task by one or two of last year's cubs, which will stay close to home and help out until they have found their own territories.

They are crepuscular (another wonderful word), which means they are largely active at dawn and dusk, which is worth noting if you want to see them. If you miss them, then you can still see where they've been as they often deposit their poo (known as scat) on mole hills or rocks. This scat is twisted, smelly and often contains the fur of the animals the fox has been eating.

Highly successful opportunists, foxes occupy a wide range of habitats. If food is plentiful, they can survive in around 25 hectares (about 62 acres in old money). However, if you get into an area where food is more scarce, such as the Scottish Highlands, their range grows massively – potentially up to 4,000 hectares.

Smaller habitats such as urban landscapes have an abundance of food and town foxes have adapted to live closely with humans, becoming far bolder than their country cousins and often venturing out during the day. But in all its guises, town and country, the fox is very much an apex predator. This is mainly because the animals that once preyed on them, including bears and wolves, are largely no longer with us, though one predator that will take a fox, given the chance, is the golden eagle.

You might think a badger would have a go, too – it is certainly strong enough – but foxes and badgers often tolerate each other to such an extent that they will share a den or sett. How the fireside chat goes I don't know, but it does seem to work.

The fox is a wily opportunist, and as such it has lent our language many descriptors. If I were to beat you in a game of draughts, for instance, you might say that I had "out-foxed" you, or call me "cunning as a fox". But the linguistic use of the word is not restricted to acts of cunning. For these are beautiful creatures, so a good-looking woman (in my cancellable generation) may be described as "foxy" (I refer you to The Doors song, *Twentieth Century Fox*).

Keen on the study of changing social mores

in linguistics (and a brave soul . . .) I set out to
see if these descriptions remain appropriate. My
findings were that women of my generation are
okay with being called a fox (some even blushed
and laughed), whereas those of a generation
younger tolerated it but don't much care for it.
Clearly, I did not ask anyone younger, as I may
have had my face slapped.

It's probably time that I put this story to
ground. I fear that I haven't quite put my finger
on the mysterious beauty of this animal, and
this is no bad thing, as if I were to succeed in
this then surely a little of their magic would be
taken away.

Suffice to say, the fox's seldom-viewed life
is something I'm always delighted to glimpse.
Whether that be a cub studying my bemused
labrador and me because the wind was coming
with it and it couldn't pick up our dangerous
scent, or the time I watched a cock pheasant
chase a big dog fox along a hedgerow. That,
and the many times I have simply watched one
moving sinuously through the countryside,

unseen (to most) and unheard. On all these occasions, my senses have become quickened and I have felt part of what is around me, rather than just an observer.

If, when the time comes, I have the honour of a brambly plot in Hartburn churchyard, I would like to think a fox might amble along to the dene to see me off. Or perhaps the foxes which do this are not so much turning up to bid farewell to those hefted to the countryside, but actually to welcome them to the next place, bright-eyed and bushy-tailed.

~

AUTHOR NOTE

Acknowledgements

It is a great adventure and a privilege to write a book. The creative process of the writing is, dare I say it, quite easy. Though without my editors Jane Pikett and Hugo Remnant I would be the owner of rough gems rather than polished stones.

The other fun bit is doing the illustrations. My art teacher Zoë Robinson has the patience of a saint and pushes me to artistic endeavours that leave me wondering, "did I really do that?"

My editor and publisher Jane Pikett and I

ACKNOWLEDGEMENTS

try with these books to create beautiful objects that are interesting to hold as well as read. Part of that magic comes from the marbling of the end pieces from master marbler Ian Varty.

Finally, I couldn't bring all this together with out the support of my family, Charlotte, Edward and Milo, and last but not least the actual writers of these stories – Ella, Frog, and Dotty the dogs.

~

Charlie Bennett

www.charliebennettauthor.co.uk

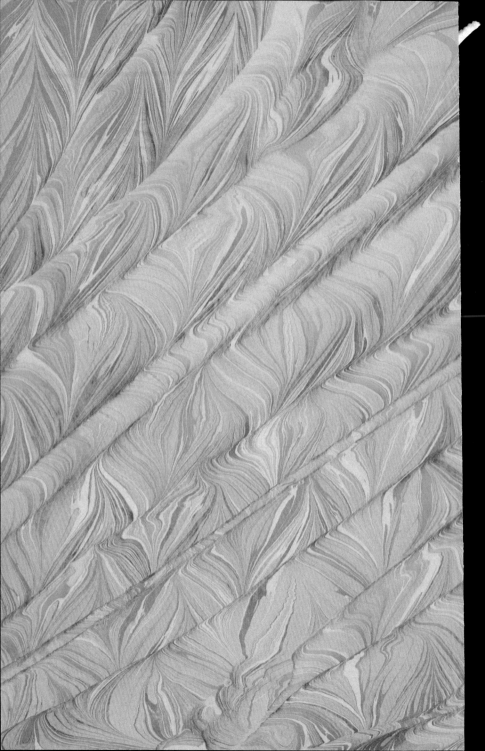